## DATE DUE

Demco, Inc. 38-293

# 100 Unforgettable Moments in
# Pro Baseball

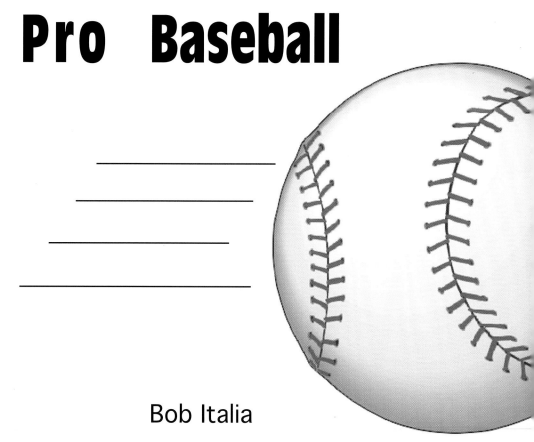

_____

_____

_____

_____

Bob Italia

ABDO & Daughters
Publishing

Published by Abdo & Daughters, 4940 Viking Drive, Suite 622, Edina, Minnesota 55435.

Copyright © 1996 by Abdo Consulting Group, Inc., Pentagon Tower, P.O. Box 36036, Minneapolis, Minnesota 55435 USA. International copyrights reserved in all countries. No part of this book may be reproduced in any form without written permission from the publisher.

Printed in the United States.

Cover Photo credits: Allsport
Interior Photo credits: Wide World Photo

Edited by Paul Joseph

**Library of Congress Cataloging-in-Publication Data**

100 unforgettable moments in pro baseball / Bob Italia.
 p.  cm. -- (100 unforgettable moments in sports)
Includes index.
Summary: Describes notable events in the history of baseball.
ISBN 1-56239-689-7
1. Baseball--United States--History--Juvenile literature.
[1. Baseball--History.]  I. Title.  II. Series: Italia, Bob, 1955-
100 unforgettable moments in sports.
GV867.5.I83  1996
796.357'0973--dc20

96-10649
CIP
AC

# Contents

# The Most Unforgettable Moment?

**M**ajor League Baseball has been around a long, long time. There have been many unforgettable moments when teams and players have performed extraordinary feats under incredible pressure. Who ever thought Babe Ruth's season record of 60 home runs would ever topple? Or Lou Gehrig's incredible games-played streak? Or Ty Cobb's mark for most career hits? These records seemed untouchable, yet a few players with immense talent and determination found ways to achieve their goals and break these records.

There is no one most unforgettable moment. The following events are in chronological order, not according to importance. The fans must decide which moments are the most memorable, for it is their enthusiasm for the game that has made baseball part of a national legacy.

*Opposite page: Mickey Mantle, the New York Yankees' slugging center fielder.*

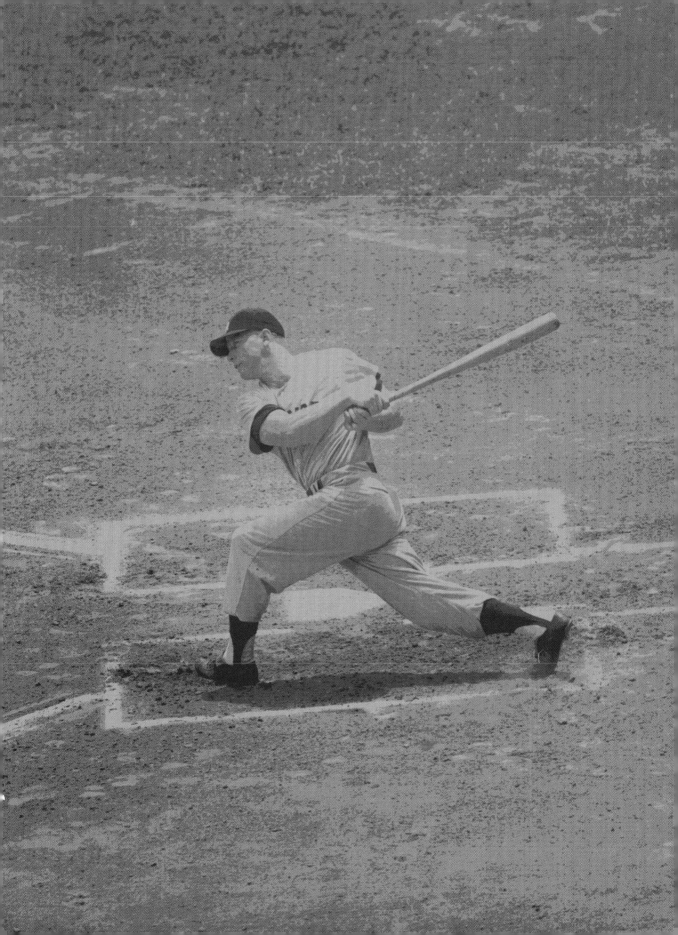

# The Babe Hits 60

In 1927, the New York Yankees won 110 games—a league record that stood until the Indians won one more in 1954. Because they were so powerful, the Yankees were known as "Murderers' Row." They batted .307 to lead the league. They also led in runs, hits, triples, home runs, slugging average, runs batted in, walks, and strikeouts. But the biggest story was slugger Babe Ruth, who was on his way to breaking his home run mark (59), set in 1921.

*Babe Ruth (right) hugging teammate Lou Gehrig.*

Ruth batted .356, drew 138 walks, scored 158 runs, and drove in 164 runs. He also had a .772 slugging percentage. No one has reached .700 in the American League since 1957.

By the end of August, Ruth had only 43 round-trippers. But in September, the Babe belted 17 homers in 27 games. On September 30—the next-to-last day of the regular season—he needed one home run to reach 60 and break the record.

Ruth stepped to the plate in the eighth inning with the score 2-2. With the count at 1-1, he sent the next pitch halfway up the right-field bleachers. The Babe circled the bases slowly as the crowd cheered. Then as he touched home plate, the fans tossed hats and confetti into the air. The Babe's 60 home runs had set the standard for baseball greatness.

Babe Ruth blasts his
60th home run of the
season in 1927.

# The Called-Shot Home Run

In the 1920s, Babe Ruth was baseball's most famous player. But in 1932, he hit a home run that turned him from a baseball great into a baseball legend.

That year, the Yankees played the Cubs in the World Series. The Yankees had won the first two Series games in New York. Now the Series came to Chicago. Nearly 50,000 jammed Wrigley Field.

The 37-year-old Ruth came up with two on in the first inning and put the Yankees ahead 3-0 with a homer into the Wrigley Field bleachers. In the fifth inning, Ruth came up with one out in the fifth. The score was now 4-4.

The first pitch was a called strike. Ruth held up one finger. After two balls, the fourth pitch was a called strike. Again Ruth held up his finger.

The next pitch never made it to the catcher's mitt. Ruth unwound his powerful body and unleashed his heavy bat. The ball sailed high into the bleachers for his second homer of the game—and the fifteenth and last of his World Series career. Ruth took his time circling the bases, taunting the Cubs' silent bench as he made his way to home plate.

Some newspapers did not mention the event the next day. But over the following weeks and months, the story grew: Did Ruth call his home run by pointing to the bleachers?

**Babe Ruth blasts a home run against the Cubs in 1932.**

The players who witnessed the event gave conflicting reports. Cubs' catcher Gabby Hartnett thought Ruth did point. So did the Yankees' Lou Gehrig, who watched the drama unfold from the on-deck circle. Yankee Joe Sewell, who batted ahead of Ruth, thought the Babe had pointed to the Cubs' bench. Cub manager Charlie Grimm thought Ruth had pointed at the mound.

Over the years, Ruth allowed the story to grow that he pointed to the bleachers. He even came up with his own version—which became more dramatic with each telling. As the years went by, there didn't seem any doubt about it: the Babe could hit a home run any time he wanted.

Whatever really happened, the question of "did he or didn't he" remains one of the greatest baseball tales in history.

# The 1934 All-Star Game

**F**ew All-Star Games have been memorable. Most are forgettable. But on July 10, 1934, something happened in the second All-Star Game that became one of the most memorable events in baseball history.

Left-hander Carl Hubbell was the starting pitcher for the National League. He would eventually finish the season with a 21-12 record and a league-leading 2.30 ERA. But few gave Hubbell much of a chance against the powerful American League lineup.

Hubbell had to face Charlie Gehringer, Heinie Manush, Babe Ruth, Lou Gehrig, Jimmie Foxx, Al Simmons, Joe Cronin, Bill Dickey, and Lefty Gomez. All were future Hall-of-Famers. But Hubbell's best pitch was a screwball—one that was unlike anything anyone had seen.

When Gehringer singled and Manush walked, it looked as if the American League would knock Hubbell from the mound. Then Babe Ruth stepped to the plate. He took three called strikes in a row and headed with a puzzled look back to the dugout.

Lou Gehrig was next. He was even more dangerous than Ruth, for he would lead the league that season with a .363 average, and would strike out just 31 times the entire year. With just four pitches, Gehrig too became a strikeout victim.

Jimmie Foxx was the next batter. He would hit .334 that year. But the screwball was too tough, and Foxx went down swinging.

Al Simmons of the White Sox led off the next inning. Simmons was a .344 hitter that year, with only 58 strikeouts. But he swung and missed three Hubbell pitches.

Joe Cronin was the next victim. He would hit .284 for the season and would strike out only 28 times. But the screwball was too much for him.

It did not take years for baseball fans to grasp the magnitude of Hubbell's feat. After all, these were legendary players—all cut down by an unassuming southpaw. After Cronin's strikeout, the fans went wild, having witnessed one of the most amazing and unforgettable moments in baseball history.

**Carl Hubbell before the 1934 All-Star Game.**

# Back-to-Back No-Hitters

In 1936, minor league pitcher Johnny Vander Meer had a 19-6 record with 295 strikeouts. He started 1937 with the Cincinnati Reds but had a 3-5 record in 19 games. So, he was sent back to the minors.

During spring training of 1938, coach Hank Gowdy told Vander Meer to watch Boston's Lefty Grove at work. Grove's style made an impression on Vander Meer, and his pitching improved. Eventually, he made the Reds' starting rotation.

On June 11, Vander Meer started a game in Cincinnati against Boston, and held the Red Sox hitless through eight innings. No Reds pitcher had thrown a no-hitter since the team's World Championship season of 1919. So in the ninth inning, the fans cheered with every pitch. Boston sent three pinch hitters to the plate, but Vander Meer retired them all. He had thrown the first no-hitter of the 1938 season.

Vander Meer's next start came at Ebbets Field in Brooklyn on Wednesday, June 15. He got six outs without allowing a base hit. Brooklyn fans started talking about another no-hitter.

Though he was not sharp, Vander Meer kept working out of jams. After eight innings, he still had his no-hitter. The Reds led 6-0.

Buddy Hassett led off the ninth for the Red Sox. He hit a slow-roller down the first-base line. Vander Meer fielded it and tagged Hassett for the out.

Vander Meer walked the next three batters for a total of eight in the game. But then Ernie Koy grounded to third, and Ernie Lombardi took the throw to get a force-out at home.

The next batter was Leo Durocher. Though a .219 hitter, Durocher could be tough at the plate. Vander Meer got two quick strikes on the batter, then put a pitch on the outside corner. It was called a ball. Durocher was still alive.

On the next pitch, Durocher lofted the ball to Harry Craft in center. He pulled it in for the final out. The crowd went wild. What pitcher today—or in the future—could possibly throw three-straight no-hitters? This is one record that may stand forever.

*Johnny Vander Meer*
*throwing his second no-hitter*
*against the Reds, 1938.*

# Lou Gehrig
# Says Good-bye

**B**ecause he played in 2,130 consecutive games, the Yankees' Lou Gehrig was known as the "Iron Horse." His streak was a record that stood until 1995 when it was finally broken by Cal Ripken, Jr.

The streak ended on April 30, 1939, in Detroit. With his batting average at .143 and his health failing, Gehrig told manager Joe McCarthy to take him out of the lineup. No one knew at the time that Gehrig would never play again.

The Iron Horse was struck down by "Lou Gehrig's disease," a serious illness that attacks the spine and causes paralysis. It is a disease which to this day remains a medical mystery.

On July 4, 1939, Lou Gehrig Appreciation Day was held at Yankee Stadium. It was one of the most emotional events in baseball history. That day, a dying Gehrig said good-bye to baseball, giving one of the most famous speeches ever.

"Today," he said, speaking into a microphone on the field, "I consider myself the luckiest man on the face of the earth." He had had a great career filled with many unforgettable moments. Nothing could ever take that away from him. Gehrig spoke his own words. He did not hire a speech-writer. The fans, though saddened, applauded his speech.

Gehrig's suffering ended on June 2, 1941, 16 years after his remarkable playing streak started. He was only 37 years old.

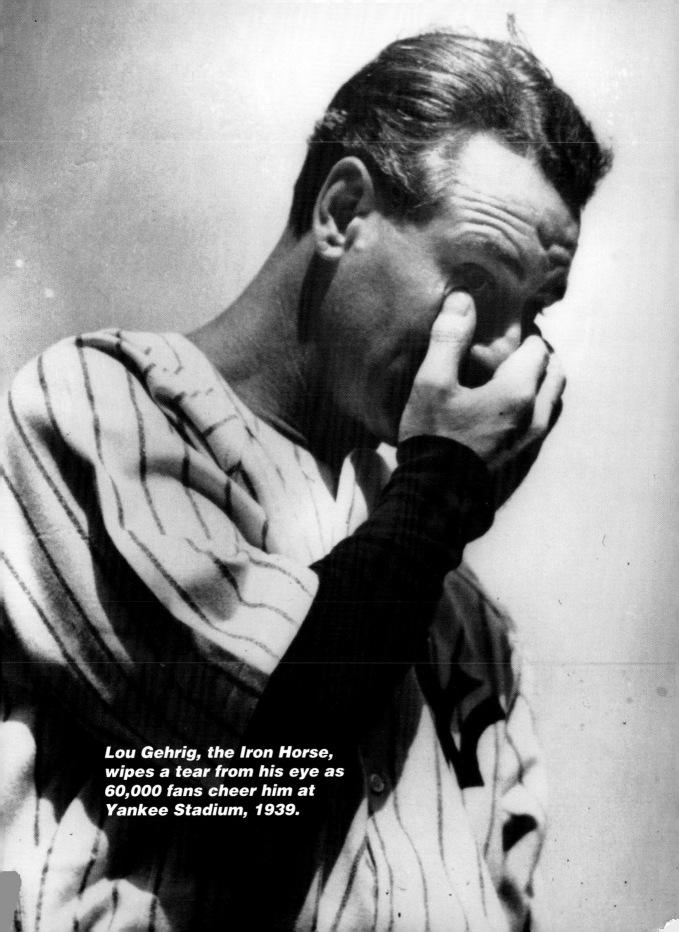

Lou Gehrig, the Iron Horse, wipes a tear from his eye as 60,000 fans cheer him at Yankee Stadium, 1939.

# The Streak

The 56-game hitting streak of the New York Yankees' Joe DiMaggio in 1941 remains one of the most impressive accomplishments in baseball history. Unlike other baseball feats, a hitting streak must be accomplished on a day-by-day basis—with no breaks—over a long period of time.

The streak started without much flair on May 15, when DiMaggio went 1-for-4 against Chicago. The streak reached 12 straight when Joe went 4-for-5. On June 2, he had hit safely in 19 straight games.

On June 8, the streak reached 23—tying Joe's best previous performance. Then DiMaggio became the first Yankee to hit in 30 consecutive games.

When DiMaggio got a hit in his 40th straight game on June 28, against Philadelphia, he equaled Ty Cobb's best mark. The next day, DiMaggio played a doubleheader and had a hit in each game. In the July first doubleheader, he went 2-for-4 in the first game to set a new league record, and 1-for-3 in the nightcap. With a homer in a game the next day, he reached 45 to break the record.

From then on, the record was all DiMaggio's. And he showed no signs of letting up. In a game against the Indians at Cleveland on July 16, Joe went 3-for-4 with a double to run the hitting streak to 56.

More than 67,000 fans turned up the next night at Cleveland Stadium. In the first inning, DiMaggio hit a shot down the third-base line, but it was backhanded by the third baseman, who threw out Joe by less than a step.

DiMaggio walked in the fourth. In the seventh, he ripped another shot to third. Again Joe was thrown out at first.

In the ninth, the Yankees held a 4-1 lead. DiMaggio stepped to the plate with the bases loaded and one out. He swung at a 2-1 pitch and grounded hard up the middle. The shortstop snagged the ball, stepped on second for the force, then threw to first to complete a double play. DiMaggio showed no emotion as he took his position in center field.

*Joe DiMaggio takes a powerful cut at the ball during his amazing streak.*

The Yankees won the game, but DiMaggio never got another chance to bat. The streak had come to an end at 56 consecutive games. During that magical time, DiMaggio batted .408 as the Yankees moved into first place, eventually capturing the pennant. In all, DiMaggio had 91 hits, including 15 homers and 55 RBIs. The next day, he began a 17-game hitting streak. When it ended, DiMaggio had hit safely in 73 out of 74 games.

# Jackie Robinson Arrives

**M**ajor league baseball had never seen a black player in the twentieth century. There was no strong pressure on team owners, who were happy to attract their small white audiences. Blacks had to play in the Negro League.

In 1943, New York Dodgers' general manager Branch Rickey began thinking of adding black players to his team—a decision that would help attendance in Brooklyn where there was a large black population. Rickey considered Don Newcombe, Roy Partlow, John Wright, Sam Jethroe, and Jackie Robinson.

*Jackie Robinson receives the Rookie of the Year Award, 1947.*

On October 23, Rickey signed 27-year-old Jackie Robinson to a minor league contract for the 1946 season. In 1945, the infielder had batted .387 with the Kansas City Monarchs of the Negro League. He also had been a four-sport star at UCLA and an army lieutenant during World War II. Most importantly, he had the intelligence and discipline that was needed to deal with the

pressures and publicity of being the first black player in an all-white league.

Robinson had no trouble with Triple A baseball. He hit .349, stole 40 bases, and led the league's second basemen in fielding. In 1947, Robinson batted .625 in seven exhibition games against Brooklyn. That's when the Dodgers announced that Jackie would join the team.

Robinson's first game—April 15, 1947—was more of a news event as 25,623 fans came to the stadium. Jackie played first base, and went hitless in three at-bats against the Boston Braves. Robinson went on to hit .297 his first year, playing in all but three games. For his efforts, Robinson won the Rookie of the Year Award, which was created that season. Forty years later, Commissioner Peter Ueberroth renamed the award the Jackie Robinson Award.

The Dodgers clinched the 1947 pennant—their first in six years. Between 1947 and 1956, Robinson helped the Dodgers to six pennants. He was the league's Most Valuable Player in 1949.

Robinson retired in 1956 with a .311 career average. For the rest of his life, he fought for equal rights, and hoped to one day see a black baseball manager. Jackie died of diabetes in 1972 at the age of 53.

# The Shot Heard Around the World

**O**n October 3, 1951, the Brooklyn Dodgers and the New York Giants finished the regular season tied for first place with 96-58 records. To decide the National League pennant, they met in a best-of-three playoff series. The two teams split the first two games, setting up the dramatic Game Three climax.

In those days, few homes had television. So many people tuned in to the radio broadcast. The Dodgers took an early 1-0 lead, but then the Giants tied it in the last of the seventh. In the top of the eighth, the Dodgers scored three times. The Giants did not score in the bottom of the eighth. It looked like the Dodgers had the pennant.

In the bottom of the ninth, the first Giant hitter, Alvin Dark, got an infield single. The next batter, Don Mueller, singled into right, sending Dark to third. Now a home run would tie the game.

Monte Irvin was next. But he fouled out. That brought up Whitey Lockman, who slammed a double to left, scoring Dark. With runners at second and third with one out, a single would tie the game.

It was Bobby Thomson's turn to bat. The first pitch was a called strike. The second one was high and inside—but Thomson turned on it. The ball rocketed toward the 315-foot sign in left.

For a moment, Giants' radio announcer Russ Hodges thought the left-fielder might make the catch. Then Hodges' voice began

**Bobby Thomson (far left at the top of the stairs) rubs the head of manager Leo Durocher.**

to get excited: "It's gonna be . . . I believe . . . the Giants win the pennant! The Giants win the pennant! The Giants win the pennant! The Giants win the pennant! Bobby Thomson hits into the lower deck of the left-field stands! The Giants win the pennant! I don't believe it! I don't believe it! I do *not* believe it!"

Fans rushed onto the field while the overjoyed Thomson hopped and jumped around the bases. With the mob of fans and teammates greeting him at home plate, Thomson had difficulty touching the base. After the long run to the center-field clubhouse, Thomson returned to the field to acknowledge the cheering fans. Thomson's home run was one of the most dramatic endings to a playoff game, and instantly became part of baseball lore.

# Willie Mays and the Catch

**W**illie Mays was one of the few sluggers in baseball history whose fielding was as good as his offense.  He made many brilliant plays in his long career—but none more famous than the over-the-shoulder running catch in the 1954 World Series.

The New York Giants faced the Cleveland Indians.  With the score 2-2, Larry Doby led off the eighth inning for Cleveland with a walk.  Al Rosen singled him to second.  Slugger Vic Wertz took the very next pitch and hit it deep to right-center field.

In the horseshoe-shaped Polo Grounds, the deepest part of center field was 490 feet—the farthest in baseball.  Instantly, Mays turned and raced at full speed with his back to the infield.  About 450 feet from home plate, Willie peeked over his left shoulder and picked up the ball.

Making a next-to-impossible catch in the World Series is always a noteworthy event.  But what Mays did turned him into a fielding legend.

In a single motion, Mays made the catch, whirled (Section 1 & 2), and fired the ball toward second base (Section 3 & 4).  Davey Williams took the throw, fired home, and held the runners.  What should have been two or three runs had been turned into none.  The catch simply broke the Indians' hearts.  The Giants won the game in the 10th inning with a homer, but Mays' brilliant catch is all that anyone remembers.

**Section 1**

**Section 2**

**Section 3**

**Section 4**

*Willie Mays and the Catch.*

# Don Larsen and the Perfect Game

The list of baseball's 15 perfect games has many well-known names, including Cy Young, Sandy Koufax, Jim Bunning, and Catfish Hunter. Don Larsen is not one of those famous names. But in October 1956, he pitched the only perfect game in World Series history.

Larsen was the starter in Game 5 for the New York Yankees and would face the Brooklyn Dodgers' Jim Gilliam, Pee Wee Reese, Duke Snider, Jackie Robinson, Gil Hodges, Sandy Amoros, Carl Furillo, Roy Campanella, and Sal Maglie. Reese, Snider, Robinson, and Campanella eventually became Hall-of-Famers.

At the start of the game, Larsen set down the Dodgers in order. By the sixth inning, the fans were talking about a no-hitter. More amazingly, not one Dodger had reached base—not on a walk or an error.

By the seventh inning, the 64,519 fans at Yankee Stadium were cheering every pitch. A perfect game was something that just didn't happen in baseball—especially in the World Series. The last one had been 34 years earlier. To get his, Larsen had to face the tough Dodger lineup one more time.

In the seventh inning, Gilliam grounded to short, Reese flied to center, and Snider flied to left. In the eighth, Robinson grounded back to the box, Hodges lined to third, and Amoros flied to center.

In the ninth inning, Larsen got Furillo on a routine fly to right. Campanella was up next. He hit a grounder to Billy Martin at second. One more batter, and the perfect game was his.

Dale Mitchell was up next. The first pitch was outside for a ball. The crowd groaned. Larsen threw a called strike to even the count. Mitchell swung and missed the next pitch, then fouled one into the left-field stands.

The next pitch was close. The umpire yelled "strike three" and ran off the field. Larsen had done it! A no-hitter, a perfect game— only the fifth of the century, and the first and only one in World Series play.

**Don Larsen pitches in the 1956 World Series.**

# Ted Williams Goes Out in Style

**V**ery few of baseball's greatest players retire at the top of their game. They often hang on one too many years, hoping to recapture the lost magic with which they once played. But no one retired with the style that Boston's Ted Williams did.

Williams was the best hitter of modern baseball—if not the best ever. He had a lifetime .344 batting average, and hit 521 home runs. Williams won seven batting titles—his first when he was a 21-year-old rookie in 1939, and one at the age of 40 in 1958. In 1941, he batted .406—the last player to top a .400 average.

In 1960—his fourth decade in baseball—Williams got off to a fast start. He hit 8 home runs in his first 15 starts, including the 500th home run of his career. He also made the All-Star team for the 16th time.

But as the 1960 season drew to an end, Williams admitted it would be his last. He kept his average over .300 and continued hitting home runs.

September 26 was Williams' final game in Boston's Fenway Park. Before the game began, it was announced that Ted's number 9 would be retired. Williams thanked the fans. Then it was time to play baseball.

Ted walked in the first inning. In his second at-bat, he hit a drive deep to center that was hauled in. In the fifth, he hit another deep drive, but the ball was caught.

Williams stepped to the plate in the eighth, with Boston trailing 4-2. The fans gave Williams one last ovation. The first pitch was a ball. The next one was a fastball, but he swung and missed. Williams looked for the same pitch again. He got it.

Williams drove the ball deep into the right field bullpen. The roar from the crowd was deafening. Boston went on to win 5-4.

After the game, the Sox announced that Williams would not go to New York with the team to end the season. The home run—number 521 in his career, and number 29 for the season—was the final at-bat of his career. No one else has ever hit as many home runs in his final year. But then again, there may never be another player like Ted Williams.

*Red Sox slugger Ted Williams.*

# Mazeroski's Homer

**A**lmost every baseball season ends the same way. A pitcher faces the year's final hitter in the World Series. The hitter makes an out, and everyone mobs the pitcher. But the 1960 season was the first to end with a home run.

The New York Yankees and the Pittsburgh Pirates faced off in the World Series. With sluggers like Mickey Mantle and Roger Maris, the Yankees looked unbeatable. But the Pirates pushed the Series to seven games.

In Game 7, Pittsburgh took an early lead. But the Yankees scored a run in the fifth and four in the sixth to take a 5-4 lead.

In the last of the eighth, the Pirates exploded for five runs— including a Hal Smith three-run homer. Three more outs and the Pirates would have their first World Championship since 1925. But New York rallied in the top of the ninth inning to tie the score.

In the bottom of the ninth, Bill Mazeroski led off for the Pirates. He was known for his fielding, not his hitting.

On the second pitch, Mazeroski took a powerful cut and sent the ball toward the left-field wall. Outfielder Yogi Berra ran back to make the catch—but watched the ball sail into the stands for a dramatic game-winning home run. Mazeroski jumped and hopped around the bases, escorted by a handful of fans who had eluded security. Never had a World Series ended in such a dramatic way.

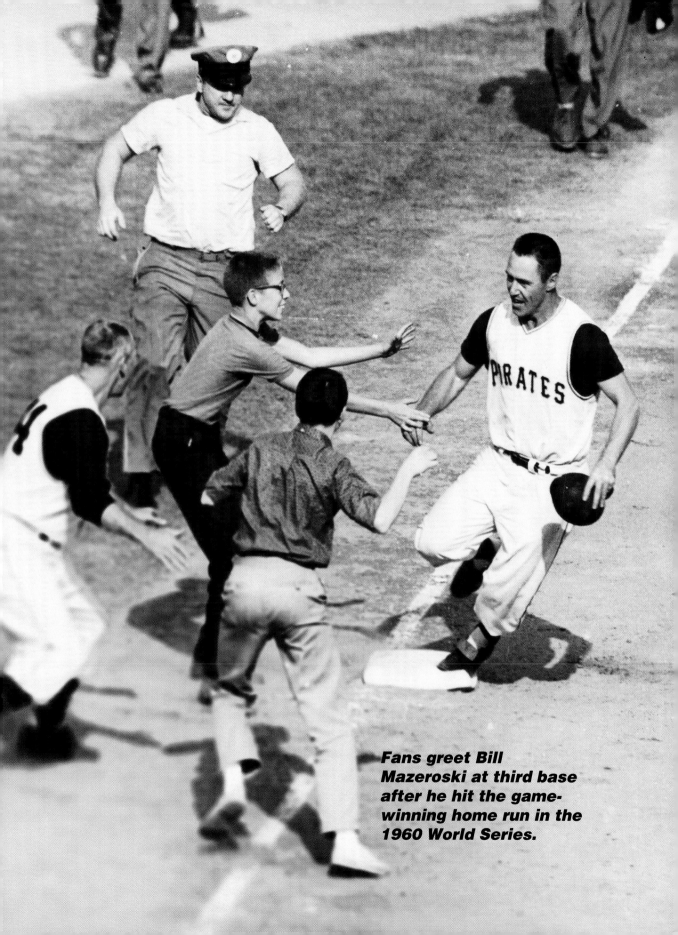

*Fans greet Bill Mazeroski at third base after he hit the game-winning home run in the 1960 World Series.*

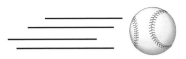

# Roger Maris
# Surpasses the Babe

**R**oger Maris' first three seasons were spent with the Cleveland Indians and Kansas City Athletics. During that time, he hit 58 home runs—a good performance, but nothing that would get him into the Hall of Fame.

The Yankees felt differently. Maris was a lefty who could reach the short right-field seats in Yankee Stadium with ease. So New York traded four players to Kansas City and obtained Maris for the 1960 season. Maris responded with 39 homers and won the league's Most Valuable Player Award.

In 1961, Maris did not hit his first home run until the eleventh game of the season. Then he and teammate Mickey Mantle started hitting them often. Newspapers around the country took notice and began running daily charts comparing their progress to Ruth's "unbreakable" record of 60.

Going into Game 154 in Baltimore, Maris needed two home runs to tie Ruth. He hit number 59, and just missed number 60. The fans applauded his effort.

The Yankees returned home, having already clinched the pennant. They would go on to win their nineteenth World Championship. But the big story was Maris, who tied Ruth at 60 on September 26, in Game 159. The injured Mickey Mantle had already finished the season with 54—a career high.

The final game of the season arrived. In the first inning, the 27-year-old Maris flied out. In the fourth, he took two balls. The 23,000 fans booed. They wanted to see him swing for the fences.

**Roger Maris bows to fans after hitting his 61st home run in 1961.**

On the next pitch, Maris obliged them. He got a fastball down the middle, and took a mighty cut. Maris stood at the plate and watched the flight of the ball. He knew that baseball history had been made. Roger Maris had become the first man in history to hit 61 home runs in a single season.

Maris rounded the bases with his head down, as if embarrassed by his amazing accomplishment. When he reached the dugout, his teammates forced him out to take a bow. The Yankees won the game 1-0. It was the team's 240th homer of the year—an all-time record. Even more, Maris had become a baseball immortal.

# Denny McLain

In 1967, pitcher Denny McLain had an unimpressive won-loss record of 17-16 on a Detroit Tiger team that finished the season 20 games over .500. But in 1968, McLain won game after game after game, and kept the Tigers on top. By midseason, fans wondered whether he could keep up the pace and become the first 30-game winner in the American League since Lefty Grove in 1930.

To win 30 games, McLain had to accomplish the impossible. The average starting pitcher got only about 35 starts a year. McLain, however, made 41 in 1968, in what became known as the "Year of the Pitcher."

The 24-year-old McLain did not buckle under the pressure. He kept his winning ways throughout the summer. Finally, on September 14, at Tiger Stadium, McLain got his chance for number 30. With television cameras everywhere, McLain nailed down the win.

McLain wasn't finished. He got another win to finish the year with a 31-6 record. He also had 280 strikeouts, a 1.96 earned-run average, and 28 complete games. In the current era of setup and relief pitchers, it is hard to imagine anyone reaching 30 wins anytime soon.

Denny McLain pitching
toward his 30th win, 1968.

# The Miracle Mets

The 1968 Mets were not a good team. They finished 24 games out of first place, which gave little reason for high expectations the following season.

But the Mets were talented. In 1969, they had pitchers Tom Seaver, Jerry Koosman, Nolan Ryan, Gary Gentry, and Tug McGraw. Koosman was the oldest at 26.

By August 16, the Mets' pitching staff had a 2.03 ERA. They reached first place on September 10. Helped by the Chicago Cubs' collapse, their gain of 12 1/2 games in September was the biggest in major league history. The Mets clinched the division title on September 24, and went on to win 100 games that miracle season.

In the League Championship Series against Atlanta, Mets' pitching mowed down the Braves in three straight. But even the most avid Mets fans figured it was all over in the World Series. New York faced a Baltimore Orioles team that had won 109 games during the regular season.

When New York lost 4-1 in Game 1, most thought the Mets' luck had run out. But the Mets didn't feel that way. They knew that good pitching could shut down any team. And they went out and proved it.

The Mets won the next game 2-1. In Game 3, they won 5-0. In Game 4, Seaver lasted 10 innings to beat Baltimore 2-1. During the game, outfielder Ron Swoboda made one of the greatest catches in World Series history, robbing Brooks Robinson of a single that could have put the Orioles ahead in the ninth. His miracle catch

**The New York Mets celebrate after winning the 1969 World Series.**

kept the game tied at 1-1. Then in the tenth, Mets' catcher J. C. Martin bunted with a runner on third. The throw to first hit Martin in the back and the winning run scored. One more victory, and the Mets were World Champions!

In Game 5, New York had the lead in the ninth inning. When Baltimore's Dave Johnson flied out to Jones in left for the final out, the stadium erupted. Just one year earlier, the Mets were one of the league's worst teams. Now they were World Series Champions.

# Hammerin' Hank

When Babe Ruth retired in 1935, his 714 career homers was a record most experts thought would never fall. Thirty years later, Ruth was nearly 200 home runs ahead of the closest challenger.

In 1965, 31-year-old Hank Aaron was 348 homers away. If he played to age 40—9 more years—he would have to average 39 a season.

Atlanta Stadium's short fences gave Aaron a chance. In his first season with the Braves, he led the league with 44 home runs. In 1967, he swatted out a league-leading 39 for a total of 481. Reaching the 500 club did not seem a problem.

In 1973, the 40-year-old Aaron showed no signs of slowing down. He had 673 through 1972—second only to Ruth, and only 41 behind him. That season, he hit 40 to give him 713 at year's end.

Early in 1974, there seemed no doubt that the record would fall. With his very first swing on opening day, Aaron belted number 714—a record that had stood in the books for 39 years.

Four days later, April 8, 1974, Atlanta played in the first "Monday Night Baseball" game before a record crowd of 53,775. They booed loudly as Aaron walked in the first inning.

In the fourth, Aaron took his second swing of the season on a 1-0 pitch. The ball soared into the Braves' bullpen. Following a long delay with ceremonies on the field, the game resumed. But many of the crowd left the stadium, having already witnessed baseball history.

The year 1973 was Aaron's last productive season. He hit 20 homers for the Braves in 1974, and then was traded to the Milwaukee Brewers where he played his two final seasons as a designated hitter, hitting only 22 homers. Aaron retired with 755 career homers. It will take 40 a year for 19 years to reach that mark, and no one is even close. But that's what was said about Ruth's record.

*Henry Aaron watches the flight of the ball after he slugs his record 715th home run.*

# Fisk Strikes at Midnight

In 1975, the Boston Red Sox were underdogs in the 1975 World Series against the "Big Red Machine" of Cincinnati. The Reds had Johnny Bench, Pete Rose, Tony Perez, Joe Morgan, and David Concepcion.

After five tough games, the Reds held a 3-2 lead and were one win away from their first World Championship in 35 years. The Red Sox had not won the Series since 1918.

Game 6 was played at night in Boston's Fenway Park on October 21. The Red Sox scored three runs in the first inning on a homer by Fred Lynn. But the Reds tied it with three runs in the fifth. Then Cincinnati scored two in the seventh and one in the eighth to take a 6-3 lead.

In the last of the eighth, the Sox staged a rally and tied the game. In the ninth, in the tenth, and in the eleventh, no one scored. The clock struck midnight. It was now October 22.

Boston catcher Carlton Fisk came to bat in the last of the twelfth inning. He hit the second pitch to left field. It was high and deep enough to be a home run—but was it fair or foul?

Fisk leaned a few feet up the line from home plate and repeatedly waved his hands toward fair territory, hoping to coax the ball over the wall. When the left-field umpire signalled fair-ball, Fenway Park erupted. Fisk jumped for joy and happily circled the bases.

*Carlton Fisk jumps for joy as he hits his twelfth-inning home run to win the sixth game of the World Series.*

It was unfortunate for the Sox that the Series did not end there. The Reds won the final game for the championship.

Fisk left the Red Sox after the 1980 season and joined the Chicago White Sox, where he played longer than he caught for Boston. But because of his dramatic and famous home run, Fisk remains an all-time favorite of Red Sox fans everywhere.

# Mr. October

**A**lthough the New York Yankees won the 1976 pennant, their four-game World Series loss convinced owner George Steinbrenner that changes were needed. So Steinbrenner began searching for players who could improve his team.

At 30 years old, slugger Reggie Jackson was at his peak. While playing for Oakland in 1969, Jackson's 47 home runs made him famous. He also contributed mightily to Oakland's division champions between 1971 and 1975. Then there was the MVP award in 1973—and a titanic All-Star Game home run in 1971 that made him a legend. He was the kind of flashy player Steinbrenner liked. So Jackson came to play for the Yankees in 1977.

Jackson played well his first season in New York. He hit 32 homers and drove in 110 runs as the Yankees won their second straight pennant. But in the American League Championship Series against Kansas City, Jackson went 1-for-15 in the first four games. The Yankees, however, still won the series and went on to face the Los Angeles Dodgers in the World Series.

Jackson emerged from his slump in the middle three games in Los Angeles. He homered in the fourth game, then launched another shot in his last at-bat in Game 5.

The Series returned to New York on October 18, with the Yankees up three games to two. The Dodgers scored two quick runs in the first inning. In the second, Jackson walked and scored on a Chris Chambliss home run that tied the score.

In the fourth, with the Dodgers leading 3-2 , Jackson came up with a man on first. He belted Bert Hooton's first pitch into the right-field seats, giving the Yankees a 4-3 lead. The scoreboard flashed "REG-GIE, REG-GIE" as the fans cheered his name.

In the fifth, Jackson stepped up to the plate. He took the first pitch, then blasted another two-run homer to right, making the score 7-3. It was Jackson's fourth Series home run. The Dodgers were stunned and would never recover. The game was now the Reggie Jackson Show— and he was about to make an encore.

**Reggie Jackson played his best in the World Series.**

Jackson came up in the last of the eighth to face knuckleball pitcher Charlie Hough. The fans stood and clapped, hoping for one more home run.

Not about to disappoint his audience, Jackson put all he had into his first swing and launched a rocket deep into center field. The blast was his third home run of the game, his fifth of the Series, and his fourth in four times at bat. That night, Reggie Jackson became "Mr. October" for his amazing performance in the World Series.

# Pete Rose

**I**n 1978, 37-year-old Pete Rose was at the top of his game. But he was 1,191 hits behind Ty Cobb's career record of 4,191. At 200 a year, Rose would have to play past age 42 to have a shot at the record.

Rose got his 3,500th hit in 1980, helping the Phillies to their first pennant in 30 years. In 1981, Rose passed Stan Musial with his 3,631st hit on August 10. Rose surpassed Hank Aaron for second place on June 22, 1982, leaving only Cobb ahead of him. In 1984, the Phillies let him go to Montreal as a free agent. There— on April 13, 1984—the 43-year-old Rose became only the second man in history to reach 4,000 hits. Still, he was 192 hits shy, and his skills were fading.

Rose was not a starting player in Montreal, and his quest for Cobb's record seemed to be at an end. But then, on August 16, Rose returned to Cincinnati to play for and manage the Reds. Rose finished the 1984 season with 4,097 career hits—just 95 short. The record was just a season away.

On Wednesday, September 11, 1985, Rose stepped to the plate before a hometown crowd of 47,237. He already tied Cobb's record of 4,191 in Chicago, and he ended the drama quickly. On a 2-and-1 pitch, Rose lashed a single to left-center. He made the turn at first, clapped his hands, and returned to the base. His teammates poured from the dugout to congratulate him.

Rose played into the 1986 season, finishing with 4,256 hits. Never announcing his retirement, he was released as a player on November 11.

Pete Rose receives a hug from Reds owner Marge Schott after breaking the record for most career hits.

# Twenty Strikeouts

**O**n April 29, 1986, the twenty strikeout mark was reached for the first time in baseball history by Roger Clemens of the Boston Red Sox. It happened at Fenway Park against the Seattle Mariners. He didn't walk a single batter that day while earning a 3-1 victory. In all, Clemens pitched nine innings, gave up three hits, one run, no walks, and recorded the twenty strikeouts—including eight in a row.

Clemens had at least one strikeout in every inning. He also retired the side on strikeouts three times. Phil Bradley went down four times, including number twenty in the ninth inning for the second out. Clemens had a shot at 21 against Ken Phelps, but he grounded out.

Will the record ever be broken? Many experts say no. But with league expansion and the dilution of talent, power pitchers such as Clemens could take the record to new heights.

*Opposite page:*
*Pitcher Roger Clemens strikes*
*out 20 batters in a single game.*

# Kirk Gibson's Home Run

The Los Angeles Dodgers were not expected to compete for the 1988 pennant. But then they signed free agent Kirk Gibson. In 150 games, he hit .290 with 25 homers and 31 stolen bases. For his efforts, the former Detroit slugger won the league's MVP Award, leading the Dodgers to the 1988 National League West title.

In the NL Championship Series, the Dodgers surprised the Mets in seven games despite a .154 series from Gibson, who was hobbled with injuries. Although he got only four hits, two were homers—including a dramatic twelfth inning game winner in Game Four.

In Game 1 of the World Series against Oakland, Jose Canseco hit a grand-slam home run off a center-field television camera in the second inning to give the A's the lead. Reserve outfielder Mickey Hatcher, playing left field for the ailing Gibson, countered with a two-run homer.

Oakland led 4-3 heading into the bottom of the ninth. The Dodgers had to face closer Dennis Eckersley, who had 45 saves in the regular season. After two quick outs, it looked like Oakland had the victory. But then Eckersley walked pinch hitter Mike Davis.

Gibson limped from the dugout and stepped to the plate. The Dodger fans went wild. He fouled off four pitches—then got one that he liked. Gibson sent a drive into the right-center field bleachers for the game-winning home run. In Game 5, the Dodgers beat the A's 5-2 to finish off the upset World Series.

*Kirk Gibson celebrates after hitting a game-winning homer in the 1988 World Series.*

# The Ryan Express

In the National League, the 300 strikeout mark was never reached until Sandy Koufax got 306 in 1963 and 382 in 1965.

In 1972, his first season with the California Angels of the American League, Nolan Ryan twice had 16 strikeouts in a game. He also had nine shutouts, a one-hitter, a pair of two-hitters, and a 1.07 ERA at home, holding opposing batters to a .143 average. And he had over 300 strikeouts.

The following season, Ryan became a 20-game winner for the first time. Even more, he became the fifth man in baseball history to hurl two no-hitters in one season. Ryan had over 300 strikeouts again—including 17 strikeouts in one game.

In his final start of the year, Ryan needed to fan 15 Minnesota Twins to tie Koufax's season strikeout record of 382. It was a tough task, but Ryan, in the eighth inning, fanned Steve Brye to tie the record. With the game in extra innings, Ryan blew three in a row past Rich Reese for strikeout number 383 of the season—a new major league record.

Nolan's third no-hitter tied Feller for the most ever pitched by one man. He then broke Feller's mark with his fourth no-hitter on June 1, 1975.

Ryan returned to the National League to play for the Houston Astros. He surpassed Walter Johnson's career strikeout total of 3,509 established in 1927. The Ryan Express kept rolling. Eventually, he passed 4,000 and 5,000. In 1981, Ryan pitched his fifth no-hitter. In his last two years with the Astros, he won two more strikeout titles.

The 42-year-old Ryan joined the Texas Rangers in 1989. He passed 5,000 strikeouts by once again reaching 300 for the season.

In 1990, Ryan led the league in strikeouts and won his 300th game. He also threw his sixth and seventh career no-hitters. Only a pitcher with enormous talent and staying power can knock Nolan Ryan from the record books.

**Nolan Ryan is carried off the field by his teammates after throwing an unprecedented seventh no-hitter.**

# Worst to First

In 1991, the Minnesota Twins rose from last place in the American League West to the top in one season, mostly because of their pitching staff. Starters Kevin Tapani, Scott Erickson, free agent Jack Morris, and closer Rick Aguilera led the way.

The Twins topped the Toronto Blue Jays to make it to the World Series against the Atlanta Braves. Minnesota took the first two games with the help of their white-towel-waving fans, who shook the Metrodome with their nonstop screaming.

Returning to Atlanta, the Braves won the third game 5-4 in 12 innings on a Mark Lemke RBI single, and the fourth game 3-2 with Lemke scoring in the last of the ninth. Game 5 was a 14-5 blowout win for Atlanta, putting the Braves up 3-2. They needed only one win in Minnesota for the World Championship. But so far, the home team had won every game.

In the sixth game, Minnesota won when Kirby Puckett belted a homer in the last of the eleventh. The seventh game would decide the champion. The Twins gave the ball to Morris.

Neither team could push home a run through nine innings. The game was still tied 0-0 when Morris took the mound in the tenth. Manager Tom Kelly wanted to lift Morris, but Jack told his manager he wanted to keep going. Kelly saw the fire in Morris' eyes, and kept him in the game. Morris then mowed down the Braves in the tenth.

*The Twins celebrate their 1991 World Championship.*

In the last of the tenth, Dan Gladden led off with a double to left-center. Chuck Knoblauch sacrificed him to third. Both Puckett and Kent Hrbek were intentionally walked to load the bases.

Gene Larkin stepped to the plate to pinch-hit. Atlanta drew in their infield and outfield in the hopes that Larkin would not hit the ball deep. But Larkin broke their hearts with a drive over the left fielder's head. Gladden watched the ball land, raised his arms, and ran home for the winning score. The Twins—last-place losers just one year earlier—were now World Champions.

# Joe Carter's Home Run

In 1992, the Toronto Blue Jays won their first World Series championship. It was an exciting moment for the team and their fans. Toronto always had talented teams, but could never seem to put it all together. In 1992, they did. So how could the Blue Jays possibly top that first World Series experience?

Toronto had the opportunity to find out. They won their division and defeated the Chicago White Sox in the American League Championship Series to earn a return trip to the World Series. This time, they would face the Philadelphia Phillies.

The Blue Jays took Game 1, but then lost in Game 2. The third game went to Toronto, 10-3, then they recorded a great comeback in Game 4. Toronto was one game away from their second-straight World Series title. But a Game 5 loss sent the Series back to Toronto.

In Game 6, a seventh-inning Phillies rally wiped out a 5-1 Toronto lead and put Philadelphia ahead 6-5. Joe Carter stepped into the batter's box with two men on in the bottom of the ninth. On a 2-2 pitch, Carter extended his long arms over the plate and launched the ball toward left field. All the Phillies could do was watch in horror as the ball cleared the wall for the game-winning home run.

The home run touched off a thunderous roar. The celebration spilled into the streets of Toronto. Carter and Bill Mazeroski were the only two players to finish the World Series with homers.

"As soon as he hit it, I knew it was gone," said Toronto pitcher Duane Ward. "Then I started playing umpire, making sure everyone could find and touch home plate."

Said Toronto outfielder Devon White: "I have never seen anything like it. It was paralyzing." And one of the most memorable moments in baseball history.

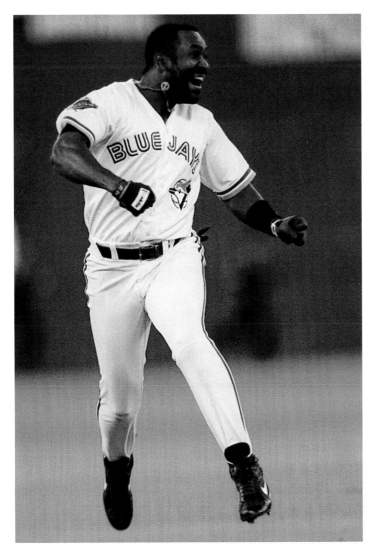

*Joe Carter jumps for joy as he rounds the bases after hitting a World Series ending home run in 1993.*

# Ironman Cal

**L**ou Gehrig's 2,130-consecutive-games-played mark was one of the most amazing baseball records ever. Most experts agreed the record would never be broken. Then Cal Ripken Jr. joined the Baltimore Orioles.

On Wednesday, September 6, 1995, Ripken tied Gehrig's 56-year-old record by hitting a home run for the second straight night and getting three hits in the Orioles' 8-0 victory over the California Angels.

The 46,804 fans at Camden Yards erupted in a five-minute standing ovation after the game became official in the fifth inning and the ten-foot high numbers on a warehouse beyond right field were flipped over to read 2,130.

Ripken's streak began on May 30, 1982, when manager Earl Weaver started him at third base, replacing Floyd Rayford in the second game of a doubleheader against Toronto. He then played in every Baltimore game in the next 13 years. But the biggest event—the record-breaker—was still to come.

Finally, it happened on September 7, 1995. When Ripken came to bat for the first time, the sellout crowd gave him a 45-second ovation. In the fourth inning, Ripken added to his heroics with a game-winning home run that helped the Orioles to a 4-2 victory.

At 9:21 P.M., the orange and black numbers posted on the warehouse behind right field at Camden Yards stopped at 2,131. At that instant, Cal Ripken Jr. broke Lou Gehrig's record.

The fans saved the longest and loudest ovation for that moment. Ripken took off his No. 8 jersey and handed it to his wife, Kelly, and children Rachel and Ryan. Ripken then shook hands with his brother Billy, his former second base partner with the Orioles. Then—for 22 minutes—the crowd cheered for Ripken, forcing him out of the first-base dugout time and time again.

At the ten-minute mark, the Orioles pushed Ripken out of the dugout. Unable to satisfy the fans with a simple dugout appearance, he trotted down the right-field foul line and began waving. Ripken cut across the outfield and high-fived a few ushers standing on the warning track. A few hands reached out of the bleachers and he slapped those.

Ripken reached left field where his trot turned into a walk. There, he slapped many more hands. He continued along the left-field stands, giving handshakes, hugs, and more slaps. Then he reached the Angels' dugout and shook hands or hugged every player.

Near the Orioles' dugout, Ripken stopped to kiss his son and daughter, then disappeared into the dugout where he grabbed a towel to wipe his face. When it was over, Ripken—like Gehrig before him—spoke humbly before the hometown crowd.

"Tonight I stand here, overwhelmed, as my name is linked with the great and courageous Lou Gehrig," Ripken told the crowd in a postgame ceremony on the field. "I'm truly humbled to have our names spoken in the same breath. As I grew up here, I not only had dreams of being a big-league ballplayer, but of being a Baltimore Oriole. As a boy and a fan, I know how passionate we feel about baseball, and the Orioles and I have benefited as a player

for that passion. I want to thank you from the bottom of my heart. This is the greatest place to play.

"This year has been unbelievable," he continued. "I have been cheered in ballparks all over the country. I give my thanks to baseball fans everywhere." Ripken then mentioned four people who influenced his life and career: his parents, former teammate Eddie Murray, and his wife.

Ripken finished the historic night by saying: "Whether your name is Gehrig or Ripken, DiMaggio or Robinson, or that of some youngster who picks up his bat or puts on his glove, you are challenged by the game of baseball to do your very best, day in and day out. And that's all that I've ever tried to do."

It will take another player with as much talent, heart, and class to break Cal Ripken's mark.

*Opposite page: Cal Ripken celebrates his record-breaking 2,131 consecutive games played streak.*

# More Unforgettable Moments

**1871**—The National Base Ball Players, the first professional league, is formed.

**1892**—Cy Young wins 36 games in 1 season.

**1896**—Hugh Jennings bats .401.

**1901**—Nap Lajoie hits .422.

**1903**—The National League and the American League become unified and the first World Series is played. Pittsburgh beat Boston 7-3.

**1904**—Jack Chesbro notches 41 wins in 1 season.

**1906**—The Chicago Cubs finish the season with a 116-36 record.

**1908**—Ed Walsh records 40 wins in 1 season.

*Ty Cobb, 1922.*

**1909**—Ty Cobb wins the Triple Crown.

**1911**—Cy Young records his 511th career win.

**1911**—Ty Cobb bats .420.

**1911**—Joe Jackson hits .408.

1912—Ty Cobb hits .410.

1913—Walter Johnson goes 36-7 with a 1.09 ERA.

1914—Nap Lajoie collects his 3,000th career hit.

1916—Pete Alexander notches his 16th career shutout.

1917—Grover Cleveland Alexander wins 30 games.

1920—Babe Ruth records an .847 slugging average.

1920—George Sisler bats .407.

1920—Bill Wambsganss completes an unassisted triple play in the World Series.

1921—Babe Ruth scores 177 runs in 1 season.

1922—George Sisler hits .420.

1922—Rogers Hornsby bats .401.

1922—Ty Cobb notches a .401 batting average.

1923—Harry Heilmann bats .403.

1924—Jim Bottomley drives in 12 runs in 1 game.

1924—Rogers Hornsby hits .424.

1925—Rogers Hornsby wins the Triple Crown with a .403 average.

*Rogers Hornsby, 1926.*

1927—Walter Johnson records his 416th career win.

1928—Ty Cobb retires with 4,191 hits.

1930—Hack Wilson hits 56 home runs with 190 RBIs.

1930—Bill Terry bats .401.

**1931**—Lefty Grove posts a 31-4 record.

**1932**—Jimmie Foxx hits 58 home runs in 1 season.

**1933**—Babe Ruth hits a home run in the first All-Star Game, won by the American League, 4-2.

**1933**—Jimmie Foxx wins the Triple Crown.

**1934**—Lou Gehrig wins the Triple Crown.

**1935**—The first major league night game is played at Cincinnati's Crosley Field.

**1936**—Ty Cobb, Babe Ruth, Honus Wagner, Christy Mathewson, and Walter Johnson are the first inductees into the Hall of Fame.

**1937**—Joe Medwick wins the Triple Crown.

**1938**—Hank Greenberg hits 58 home runs in 1 season.

**1941**—Ted Williams wins the All-Star Game with a dramatic home run.

**1942**—Ted Williams wins the Triple Crown.

**1946**—Bob Feller posts 348 strikeouts in 1 season.

**1947**—Ted Williams wins the Triple Crown.

*Pitcher Sandy Koufax, 1965.*

**1950**—Ralph Kiner slams 47 home runs in 1 season.

**1952**—Stan Musial notches his 17th straight .300+ season.

1953—The New York Yankees win their fifth straight World Series.

1954—The Cleveland Indians post a 111-43 record.

1956—Mickey Mantle captures the Triple Crown with a .353 average, 52 home runs, and 130 RBIs.

1958—Major League Baseball arrives on the West Coast as the Brooklyn Dodgers and New York Giants move west.

1958—Ernie Banks hits 47 home runs in 1 season.

1959—Pittsburgh's Harvey Haddix hurls 12 perfect innings against Milwaukee-then loses in the 13th inning, 1-0.

1965—The first indoor baseball game is played in Houston at the Astrodome.

1965—Sandy Koufax strikes out 382 batters in 1 season.

1966—Pitcher Tony Cloninger hits two grand slams in one game.

1966—Frank Robinson wins the Triple Crown with a .316 average, 49 home runs, and 122 RBIs.

**Roberto Clemente, 1967.**

1967—Carl Yastremski wins the Triple Crown.

1968—Jim Northrup hits two grand slams in one game.

1968—Don Drysdale pitches 58 consecutive scoreless innings.

1968—Bob Gibson strikes out 17 batters in the first game of the World Series.

1970—Frank Robinson hits two grand slams in one game.

1970—Tom Seaver strikes out 10-consecutive batters in 1 game—19 overall.

1971—Roberto Clemente bats .414 in the World Series.

1974—The Oakland Athletics win their third-straight World Series.

1975—Frank Robinson becomes the first African-American manager in baseball history.

1976—Mike Schmidt hits four home runs in one game.

1979—Thirty-nine-year-old Willie Stargell leads the Pirates to a World Series Championship.

1982—Rickey Henderson breaks Lou Brock's record of 118 stolen bases in a single season with 130 steals.

1982—Steve Carlton wins his record-fourth NL Cy Young Award.

1985—Vince Coleman steals 110 bases in 1 season.

1986—The Mets defeat the Houston Astros 7-6 in 16 innings to capture the National League pennant.

*Pitcher Orel Hershiser, 1988.*

1988—Orel Hershiser hurls 6 consecutive shutouts, totaling 59 consecutive scoreless innings.

1990—Cecil Fielder hits 51 home runs in 1 season.

1990—Bobby Thigpen records 57 saves in 1 season.

# Index